Squirrels

Bushy-Tail Scampers!

Dr. Richard A. NeSmith

Love of Nature Series

ISSUE 7

Applied Principles of Education & Learning

APE-Learning

FLESCH-KINCAID GRADE LEVEL: 8.2

Squirrels
(Sciuridae *sciurus*)

Almost everyone has seen or watched squirrels. They are ever before us, and being diurnal (day creatures) like us, often encounter them. They are most active during the day, and even in winter, will often venture out around noon to take advantage of the sun's warmth. Eastern grey squirrels and fox squirrels (sometimes called Sherman's or Bryant's fox squirrel) are not very aggressive. Most of us tolerate

them, and even the squirrels seem to endure us quite well. Would you believe that your local "community-dwelling" squirrels get to know you?

It seems that people either love them or disdain them.

People seem to consider them fluffy and fun or pests and "tree rats." They are related to mice and rats (Order

Rodentia), but we will learn that they are far more than just rodents. They are intelligent, social, and generally help propagate forests.

Squirrels are mammals from the Class Sciuridae, meaning *shadow tail*. Like all mammals, they breathe air and give birth to live babies rather than laying eggs. There are over 200 species (some say 267) of squirrels throughout the world. They are categorized into three types: tree, ground, and flying squirrels. Of a large number of species, five reside in the United States. These include the gray, fox, red, flying, and ground squirrels. Most squirrels in North America make their homes in trees, but some live entirely on the ground.

Because there are so many squirrel species, others will be discussed in a forthcoming issue of the *Love of Nature* series. In this issue, we will focus primarily on the **eastern gray squirrel** (*Sciurus carolinensis*) and the **fox squirrel** (*Sciurus niger*). They have so many similarities, but they are different *species,* so, by definition, they do not interbreed (or at least we have no evidence of hybrids). They are both tree-

dwelling squirrels that do not walk but **scamper** (*to run with quick, like steps, primarily through fear or excitement*) about, whether on the ground or climbing a tree. They move in small leaps and bounds.

Range

The gray and fox squirrels are native (*endemic*) to North America. That does not mean that they are native to all regions within the continent in which they might now be living. In other words, many factors can cause these movements, some natural and some human-made. One species will often become introduced (either by escaping, being set free, or by migration driven by natural changes in climate, food, or environment). This release can lead to one species slowing moving into another's natural range or territory. This mobility creates issues and new problems and can cause alarm among the environment of the original inhabitants. As one species begins intruding into another's territory, competition and disease can significantly affect the established species. The

problem becomes one of stress on one species over another due to competition over food, space, resources, and diseases.

It appears that with climate change occurring, we see this become more dynamic than previously known in our modern era. Another factor to consider whenever dealing with "common" names is that they are not always clearly

defined. For example, the *eastern* gray squirrel can be found in the Western United States. This squirrel, though, should not be confused with a larger cousin, the *western* gray squirrel (which is an entirely different species, *Sciurus griseus*). And, we will see, the eastern gray squirrel is not always wholly gray. The point here is that this is the main reason scientists and biologists adhere to identifying animals by their *genus species* to avoid such confusion or ambiguity.

Eastern "gray" squirrels can have fur coats of black, white, or blond. But they can be distinguished from fox squirrels by their white abdomens and silver, white-tipped tails. Both eastern gray and fox squirrels have brownish blotches throughout their gray fur. Fox squirrels are characteristically *larger* than eastern gray squirrels, with a

more rounded face. Their stomachs are light tan (some are almost white) to cinnamon orange. The hair on the tail's tips is orange, which will distinguish it from a gray squirrel.

Eastern Gray Squirrel

Gray squirrels are bushy-tailed rodents with a mixture of brown, black, and white fur, which, when viewed from a distance, blend to look gray. Their belly fur is white or light gray. The tail is flattened, bushy, and gray with silvery-tipped hairs.

The native eastern gray squirrel and the fox squirrel are both the most successful in adapting to urban and suburban settings. They have adjusted well to human surroundings, as well as being prolific in forested woodlands. In the wild, eastern gray squirrels can be found inhabiting large areas of mature, dense woodland ecosystems, generally covering 100 acres (40 hectares) of land.

Like the eastern gray, the fox squirrel is environmentally essential to the environment by helping trees and other plants grow, keeping the forest healthy. Some have suggested that gray squirrels may also damage (and kill) forest trees in some regions, hindering foresters from

growing high-grade hardwoods.

The range of these two squirrel species seems to be dependent on the habitat in which they live. Urban squirrels (or those in community parks) may have a smaller range than squirrels living in more natural habitats. *They are abundant in city parks, suburbs, and rural woodlands, where there are plenty of nut trees.* In natural settings, the range of several acres tends to overlap with the range of other squirrels. Although they seldom travel farther than 200 yards from home in any regular season. With that in mind, a particular squirrel could have a local range from 200-300 yards (180 – 275 meters) to as much as 5 acres (2.0 hectares). Food, trees, and predator population would all play into one's territory size.

Fox Squirrel

The fox squirrel is the largest species of tree squirrel native

to North America. They have a reddish-rusty belly and a black outline on their tail. They are larger than the eastern gray squirrel and average 17.7-27.6 inches (45-70 cm) with a tail length of 7.9-13.0 inches (20-33 cm). They range in weight from 1.1-2.2 pounds (500-1,000 grams).

Coloration is linked to geography. For example, the fox squirrel's upper body is brownish-grey to brownish-yellow, with a typically brownish-orange underside. In comparison,

the fox squirrels in the eastern regions (i.e., Appalachians) have more outstandingly dark brown and black bodies with white bands on the face and tail. And, in the south, fox squirrels can be found in isolated communities with uniform black coats. Like the eastern gray squirrel, males and females are about the same size.

Characteristics

It has been mentioned that both of these squirrel species have territories. However, those territories are only mildly marked and defended. Often their territories overlap, and they are generally more social instead of their very territorial red squirrel cousins. They tend to be content to feed among one another. Occasionally, territorial issues or disputes typically involve breeding season or stealing nuts and acorns from another's cache. Though neither the gray nor the fox squirrel is aggressively territorial, there is a *dominance hierarchy.* They'll defend their nests, food, or area. This_hierarchy can often be observed. Squirrels will chase or nip at other squirrels that are feeding in their "territory." The up-and-down and spiraling pattern around a tree

exhibited during some chases is a definite sign of a territorial dispute.

When not searching or burying food, squirrels spend their idle time in their nest, or they may lie atop a tree branch. Squirrels, in general, seem to have a preference for specific tree species in their given habitat. However, the number of such trees is quite large and includes up to 255 different types.

Squirrels have extraordinary memories, practice some unique deceptive measures, and use their tails as signaling devices. Documented studies have found squirrels *remembering* human beings. Even wild squirrels quickly learn to consider that some individuals can be risk-free and trusted sources of food. Whether they remember facial features or other recognition cues is unknown. Still, they certainly determine early on who is safe and who is not. It's true.

Squirrels carefully observe the movement and actions of people. They tend to become attached to specific individuals. Those who have raised baby squirrels have found that the male squirrels are one-person animals and quickly become attached to their human caretaker (*momma*). As pets, they tend to choose one person over the rest of the family. They then either tolerate or dislike the other family members.

Even the wild squirrels will quickly come to recognize individuals so that they no longer feel disturbed by their

My son, Wendell, making a new friend in a Mexico City park.

presence. They get to know individuals by their actions. They know who feeds them, who chases them, and whom to avoid.

Squirrels are extremely intelligent creatures and can even practice an elaborate form of deception called *bogus food burying*. Here, they act like they are digging a hole to bury an acorn or similar food item. But upon noticing another squirrel or onlooker watching, they pretend to hide and cover it up, all the time securely holding the hidden acorn in its mouth. They then scamper off to another, more secluded location and bury the cache of food. The onlooker will often go to the empty covered hole seeking to steal the acorn, only to find nothing.

There seems to be a reasonable means of communication that occurs between squirrels using their tails. Again, studies were conducted, first utilizing a squirrel museum skin with a robotic tail. They later found that only the tail was needed to convey the messages to neighboring wild squirrels. The bushy tail acts as a *signaling device*, twitching it when anxious to alert other squirrels of potential danger. The direct message a squirrel sends with its wagging tail is a warning. If they see something dangerous or suspicious, they wag their tails to alert other squirrels. They also use it to let predators know they've seen the danger, taking away the element of surprise. There seem to be other friendly and unfriendly gestures not entirely understood yet that convey meaning to their kind by swishing that bushy-tail.

Squirrels do have keen eyesight, hearing, and smell. Their peripheral vision is as good as their focal eyesight. In other words, their normal, straightforward vision is just as good as the peripheral vision, and it is all visible at once, unlike

our own vision. So, they can see what is above and beside them without moving their heads, making it hard to sneak up on them without notice. They continually listen in on the casual chirp and chatter of birds to decide when it's safe enough to be out in the open and foraging for food. Their sense of smell is keen, which they use to help locate food they've hidden away. They can smell food under a foot of snow and will dig a tunnel to retrieve it. They can also pick up information about their fellow squirrels by smelling them. Despite their association with nuts, squirrels are *omnivores* (eat both plants and animals).

Finally, when talking about a squirrel's intelligence, we cannot leave out their ability to find the nuts and acorns they bury before the winter season. This *scatter-hoarder's* ability, as it is called, was put to the test by several different researchers. In one case, acorns had embedded transmitters placed in them and were provided for a specific squirrel. He did his job and buried them. The same squirrel was then captured and held in a "Squirrel Hilton Inn" for a few months (well-cared-for). It was discovered that the buried acorns stayed in place and were not found by other squirrels. The original squirrel was returned to his tree and his territory. Upon a period of observation, that squirrel had located, retrieved, and eaten a large percentage of the

electronically monitored acorns.

The returned squirrel had found the locations where he had initially buried his cache of acorns. The conclusion was that the squirrel had an outstanding memory. It was further determined that squirrels use a *3-point triangulation method* to relocate their buried food. In other words, upon burying an acorn, the squirrel would mentally note the location of the burial in conjunction with two different objects, like a rock and a tree. The result is that it can locate what they buried using those mental references (coordinates). Not all of the acorns were found, but a large percentage of them were.

Diet

Both the fox squirrel and the eastern gray squirrel begin with 6 baby teeth and 22 permanent teeth, with an extra premolar on each side. The baby teeth are lost around 4 to 5 months of age. The four incisors (front, sharp, cutting teeth) continually grow in a continuous curved growth pattern throughout their entire lives (about 6 inches or 16 cm per year). Because they are always continuously chewing and gnawing, the continual incisor growth still provides a razor-sharp edge. If in captivity, like gerbils, they would have to be trimmed every four to six weeks unless provided proper gnawing opportunities. This can still occur in the wild, where the incisors can grow until the squirrel cannot eat anymore, and then the teeth pierce the opposite jaw, causing death.

Upon closer inspection, one can see that there is an orange tint on the teeth. The front incisors may be a darker orange color than that on the other whiter back teeth. This discoloration is due to more durable iron-enriched enamel. This enables the squirrel to cut through hard shells rather easily. The teeth in the back of the mouth are softer, causing uneven wear, which gives the teeth a sharp chisel shape. Thus, the squirrel is equipped with very razor-like, cutting-like, continually growing upper and lower incisors. These sharp incisors are softer, with an effective cutting edge, enabling the squirrel to pierce nuts and other foods. The additional space between the incisors and the molars allows a squirrel to gnaw easily.

It is common to see gnawed acorns, husks, or other nutshells littering the ground in a forest or park. In the winter, visible holes can be seen in the ground, and holes in the earth in the spring, where squirrels dug up their winter reserve of acorns. Also, they gnaw on tree trunks and limbs with their growing teeth.

They eat nuts and acorns from oak, beech, walnut, and hickory trees and seeds. They also consume buds and flowers of trees, roots, fungi, and, of course, the urban ones steal what they can from bird feeders. Being omnivores, they also eat insects and eggs. Though it is not uncommon for them to eat meat, they thrive on a diet of fruits, fungi, and seeds. Like rodents, they have been known to eat frogs, snakes, rats, bird eggs, and baby birds. If available, they will also eat farm crops such as corn and wheat. Finally, they will, like many rodents, become cannibalistic and eat their own. Either consuming their young or eating carrion (flesh of dead animals). When food is plentiful, a male (*boar*) squirrel might kill a rival male's offspring. During estrus, the sows' scent will attract males from as far away as 1,640 feet (500 meters), about the distance of 5 American grid-iron football fields.

Squirrels are seldom seen drinking water. They do tend to get their hydration from eating insects, meat, and bones. But, during periods when mommas nurse their young, extra water is needed. They will generally drink standing water, which might come from streams, ponds, puddles, or small pools of water collected in tree holes during rains.

Habitat

North American squirrels prefer stands of hardwood trees

a slightly dense understory. Eastern fox squirrels are most

abundant in *open forest* stands with less brush vegetation. In other words, most squirrels do not prefer to live in *dense* undergrowth. Trees provide these squirrels with acorns, hickory nuts, and beechnuts, which make up the bulk of their diet. Fox squirrels are also known to live among hedges and timbered fence rows next to prairies. Such habitats are also found in urban areas.

Like the eastern gray and the fox squirrel, tree squirrels live mostly high up in the trees. A group of squirrels is called a *scurry* or *dray* (drey). They build two types of nests: **tree dens** (called *dreys* or *drays*) and **leaf nests**. Male and female squirrels of all ages contribute to the building of dens.

Tree dens

Drey nests are built in the forks of trees on exposed tree branches at a safe distance above the ground, typically 60 feet (18.3 m) up. Dreys are frequently built of woven, live green twigs and lined with moss plants, thistledown, dry leaves, bark, and lined with grass and feathers. On top of this, soft compressible materials like moss and damp leaves are added. Tree cavities offer protection from weather fluctuations and access to food.

The drey/tree den is more stable and better protected within the hollow trunks of trees or natural tree cavities. They also have been known to take shelter within abandoned bird nests, such as old woodpecker holes.

This den is used year-round, but is vitally important and necessary during the winter months. Adults typically have at least two different tree dens within their home range. When a female squirrel has mated in the summer, she may return to the tree den where her winter litter was born, or more likely, she will find a new location for each litter. Adults may rotate between as many as three nests, depending on the population density where they live. These nests are usually occupied either by a single adult squirrel or by a mother and her young. *Litters born in tree dens are much more likely to survive than those born in leaf nests.*

Leaf nests

Leaf nests (sometimes called "cavity nests") are generally built in the *summer* by entangling together small branches

they have gnawed off of trees. These are built lower to the ground than the den nest, up to 30 feet off the ground in the fork between a tree limb and the tree's main trunk, well hidden by the summer greenery. A single entrance is concealed, facing the trunk of the tree. These nests are typically intended for one squirrel. Still, occasionally, two squirrels sleep together in the same leaf nest if the temperature falls.

Squirrels use these nests as *temporary shelters*, and most adults have more than one in case of insect infestation. If the nest

becomes infested with fleas or mites or disturbed by predators, the squirrel moves on to a different location and builds a new nest. Adult squirrels typically can build a nest in a single day.

Behavior

One of the most important adaptations of the gray and the fox squirrel is their ability to leap trees and the ability to get away from predators. Its adaptation for food gathering, storing, and then retrieving is extraordinary. The teeth chiseling and cracking enables them to obtain food from hard shells quickly. The squirrel's sharp claws allow it to climb trees easily and dig and grasp things with coordinated exactness.

Some squirrels are *crepuscular* (active at dusk and dawn; twilight). Most squirrels are busy all day, especially during the fall and spring months, when they are more aggressive searching for food.

Squirrels are mammals. And just like humans, squirrels experience and demonstrate emotions. It is believed that squirrels can feel happy, angry, curious, and frustrated. Squirrels are also extremely clever and will tirelessly search

for and find any means to gain entrance into garages and human homes. Gray squirrels are particularly good at finding a tiny gap and will dig under a fence.

Squirrels lick and nibble a lot. It is their way of showing affection. They also hold on to fingers and ears, etc. Their anger is indicated by a rasping growl, a chattering of teeth, and a foot stamping. But the key to interpreting their emotions may also lie somewhere else: in the curve of their majestic, bushy tails, which they can flip in a dozen different manners. They wag their tails when they are startled or alarmed, or when upset, such as if a person gets too close to their squirrel babies (kits). Tail wags also let other squirrels know if they've encroached on someone else's territory.

Squirrels are very responsive and alert, and masters of climbing. Upon close observation, one can see that squirrels leap up a tree, grabbing with front and back paws, much as they do when scampering across the ground. Part of this agility is the adaptation of the paws. They have four toes on the front foot, five on the back. The rear ankles can

rotate 180° just like that of a raccoon's. This double-jointedness enables the squirrel to grab onto the tree bark with its back feet. It can hang down head-first, or it can climb down headlong.

This sure-footedness makes them lightning fast going up, down, or around trees. However, this is not foolproof, and sometimes squirrels slip or misjudge a distance of a jump and fall. Squirrels can survive a fall at their *terminal velocity*. This term means that the animal's weight falling at its fastest rate versus the air resistance created would not cause enough force hitting the ground to kill him or her. Squirrels, then, can almost fall at any distance and survive. For squirrels, falls are not typical causes of death.

Squirrels with their fluffy, bushy tails are used to *balance* while traveling through treetops and running along electrical powerlines. The tail can also serve as a parachute to slow the fall rate and generally falls of up to 100 feet

(30.5 m) without injury. Squirrels can also change position rather quickly during a fall to ensure the best possible landing for survival.

Squirrels have a significant ecological role in the forest ecosystem, especially in their contribution to shaping plant composition. They have a peculiar habit of taking seeds, their primary source of nutrients, and burying them. They re-collect about 74% of the nuts they hide. That means that more than one-fourth of nuts and seeds buried and cached by squirrels are left to germinate. That is a significant contribution to new tree introduction and sapling growth. Misplacing or forgetting so many acorns is likely responsible for oak forest regeneration. This ecological concept is known as *seed dispersal.* The same concept holds when squirrels eat truffles (mushrooms). They help distribute truffle fungal spores.

Reproduction

Female squirrels, called *sows*, will mate with males (boars) to produce a litter of babies called kits or kittens. Squirrels can breed all year long; however, mating generally occurs in two seasons: from December to February and May until June. Females can begin to have babies at six months old and have one or two litters per year. Usually, one to four young are born in each litter, but the largest possible litter is eight. The **gestation** (pregnancy) period is about 44 days.

All squirrels are born hairless, so identifying types of tree squirrels cannot be done by sight until the tail fur emerges. Sows will nurse their babies for about two months and then could have a second litter before winter, though not always.

By week four, the babies' eyes open; by week six, the young are leaving their nest. By the time they reach eight or

nine weeks of age, baby squirrels are no longer nursing and are generally able to survive independently in the wild. During these months, the sow is very territorial and will fight to the death to defend her space. Most sows are vicious when protecting their babies.

If needed, sows will move their kits by the scruff of the neck, even if it means from one tree to another. Generally, Kits do not leave the nest until fully furred and able to survive on their own. Most kits are about the same size, and most leave the nest in April or May.

The average life expectancy for a gray or fox squirrel at birth is 1-2 years. Baby squirrels are at their peak of vulnerability. Most baby squirrels fall prey to predators and never make it to adulthood. Only about 26 percent of the *juveniles* survive their first winter. The average lifespan of an *adult* squirrel is closer to 6 years. Some squirrels in captivity have been known to live from 12 to 20 years of age, with gray squirrels having a slightly shorter lifespan.

Miscellaneous

We know that squirrels communicate with one another using their bushy tail. But they also have sounds they make to convey messages. Squirrels have their own language of chirps, moans, and tail flicks. Their chatter sometimes sounds like they are scolding a dog or us, but most of those sounds are alarm signals given to warn off a predator or to warn other squirrels of danger. In some cases, they make a crying noise when hurt or injured. Different squirrel species make different sounds, so they may not always mean the same thing.

At the end of a summer season, squirrels are often seen rolling around on the ground, biting themselves, or just acting plain crazy. An increase in temperature naturally correlates with an increase in insect populations. Such wild, crazy-acting squirrels suffer from skin irritations due to parasitic fleas, botfly larvae, and mange (caused by the

infestation of tiny mites). These can cause sores and loss of hair.

Squirrels do have a large number of predators. These include birds of prey (especially owls and hawks), automobile roadkill, snakes, weasels, wolves, coyotes, foxes, bears, bobcats, panthers, and even domesticated dogs and cats. *Owls are such a squirrel's nightmare* that placing a decorative owl decoy in one's garden tends to reduce the number of squirrels in the vicinity. It has been found that periodically moving around the decoy is needed, or else the squirrels will get wise to it.

Barking dogs tend to keep most squirrels at a distance. Some gardeners have had success in reducing squirrels by sprinkling Cayenne Pepper, red pepper flakes, paprika, or other combinations of spicy seasonings around the base of plants. Others have found it helpful to include strong-

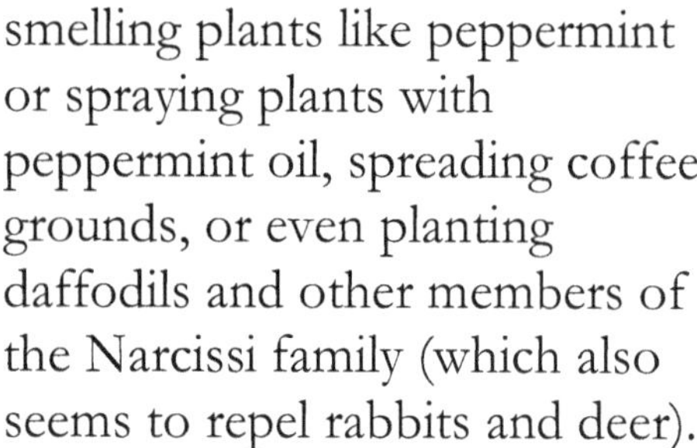

smelling plants like peppermint or spraying plants with peppermint oil, spreading coffee grounds, or even planting daffodils and other members of the Narcissi family (which also seems to repel rabbits and deer).

In some areas, humans hunt squirrels. In some states, they have a significant economic value, such as in Mississippi, where 2.5 million are harvested each year, creating an impact of over 12.5 million dollars. Disease, starvation, predators, and harsh weather are other *significant causes* of death. Squirrels dying in these ways are likely to die in their nests or otherwise hidden places, as it is unusual to see a dead squirrel carcass except in roadkill.

It should be mentioned that these natural (and unnatural) changes in population migration are not ones of battle or hostile takeovers. For example, in the eastern gray and fox squirrel populations, these two seldom interact with one another at all. They do not share the same habitat, and when they do, they do not interbreed. There are often overlapping territories, and as environmental conditions favor one species over another, the populations shift.

Squirrels are great fun to watch. They can be endearing, entertaining, and even a little enchanting. They are protected by wildlife conservation and exotic pet laws and should be respected as wild animals, despite their cuteness. Most squirrels, since they are naturally wild animals, are not available as pets.

Though most of us do, at times, feed them, it is not in their best interest or health to be supplied by humans. It alters their diet, their behavior, and their chances of survival. Squirrels dependent on handouts typically do not forage on natural food sources as do those not human-fed. Health issues can arise from improper nutrition. Also, as with all wild animals fed by humans, they can lose their natural fear of people when they begin to associate people with food.

Realize that a squirrel might follow you out of curiosity (how flattering!). Still, because their smell is very well developed, they can sense you are carrying food with you. If you do not give them any food, they will lose interest and stop following you.

Squirrels are carriers of diseases. The eastern grey squirrel, for example, can be carriers of the pox virus, which has no effect on them but will kill a red squirrel within 14 days of infection. Some of the more common infections include tularemia, typhus, plague, and ringworm. Such diseases are transmitted through bites or other forms of direct contact with infected squirrels.

Squirrels can chew through wood, plastic, rubber, and even metal with their strong teeth. These pests can deliver painful bites that draw blood. While healthy squirrels will not bite unless provoked, these animals are *susceptible* to rabies. Though squirrels, like hamsters, guinea pigs, gerbils, and other small mammals, rarely get infected with rabies, there is always a possibility, so err on the side of caution. Still, if these pests charge or attack without reason and bite, the bite must be checked by a medical doctor.

REVIEW

1. What are the two squirrels focused on in this book?

2. For what is the American tree squirrel best known?

3. What does *scamper* mean?

4. Explain how squirrels communicate with their tails.

5. What kind of food do North American squirrels prefer to eat?

6. How does a tree squirrel find the buried nuts it saved?

7. What are the major differences between an eastern gray squirrel and a fox squirrel?

8. What predator do squirrels most fear?

9. How can squirrels run down a tree?

10. What kind of predators do squirrels face?

11. How is a tree den different from a leaf nest?

12. What signs might exist to indicate that a squirrel might be infected with rabies?

EASTERN GRAY SQUIRREL

COLORING PAGE

http://www.supercoloring.com/coloring-pages/eastern-gray-squirrel

Squirrels: Bushy-Tail Scampers

Carefully read the statement or clue given and place the correct letters in the boxes.

signal   tails   species   burying   intelligent   remember   owl   fox   larger   leaf   shadow

triangulation   drey   rodentia

Across

2. Eastern gray squirrels have white abdomens and silver, white-tipped ________

4. Squirrels are extremely ______________ creatures

7. Squirrels __________ human beings.

8. The word 'squirrel' means ______ tail.

9. New low in the tree, usually 30 feet from ground is called a ________ nest.

11. Possibly a squirrel's worse enemy is the ______.

12. Squirrels seem to help forest grow by __________ seeds.

14. What Order are squirrels classified in by biologists?

Down

1. Fox squirrels are ________ than eastern gray squirrels.

3. Squirrels use their tails to ____________.

5. 3-point triangulation is a way squirrels __________ where their acorns are buried.

6. Nest high in the tree-top is called a ______ nest or den.

10. Two types of squirrels discussed in this book are the eastern gray and the ______ squirrel.

13. Eastern gray squirrels doe not interbreed with fox squirrels because they are a different ________.

INTERESTING SOURCES TO CONSIDER

10 Squirrel Facts You Didn't Know Before. Wildlife X Team International. Available at: https://www.youtube.com/watch?v=jJo48vN8rvA&t=2s

13 Things You Didn't Know About Armadillos. Available at: https://www.treehugger.com/things-you-didnt-know-about-armadillos-4869732

18 Things You May Not Know About Squirrels. Tree Hugger. Available at: https://www.treehugger.com/happy-squirrel-appreciation-day-4868817

65 Species of Squirrels in United States. Animal Lover: Available at: https://www.youtube.com/watch?v=uQNno0yFaMM

Deep Dive: What is Symbiosis? War between tree and squirrel! Stated Casually. Available at: https://www.youtube.com/watch?v=N5G0Rs8AbAo

Eastern Gray Squirrel Documentary. Available at: https://www.youtube.com/watch?v=vFQzaK3p_O0

Learn about the eastern fox squirrel in Utah on Squirrel Appreciation Day. Natural History Museum of Utah. Available at: https://www.youtube.com/watch?v=WAqFHuWG5I0

Nat Geo Wild Super Squirrel Opening Scene. Available at: https://www.youtube.com/watch?v=kOUPb1XP9vE

Squirrel Facts Mini Documentary HD. Studio Flat Productions. Available at: https://www.youtube.com/watch?v=DFcV1DxN0oU

Squirrels Just Wanna Have Fun. America's National Parks. Available at: https://www.youtube.com/watch?v=aDi8VWE4Cq8

Squirrels. National Geographic. Available at: https://www.nationalgeographic.com/animals/mammals/group/squirrels/

Squirrels: Diet, Habits & Other Facts. Live Science. Available at: https://www.livescience.com/28182-squirrels.html

Squirrels: HaveAHeart. Available at: https://www.havahart.com/squirrel-facts

Squirrels: The Human Society. Available at: https://www.humanesociety.org/animals/squirrels

ABOUT THE AUTHOR

Richard NeSmith is a native of Florida, USA. He grew up wading through the swamps of central Florida with his two younger brothers during the pre-Disney era, and unknowingly, falling in love with biology, wildlife, and nature. He has lived in seven American states, twice in Australia, and once in Mexico City. He holds eight university degrees and has taught for 14 years in secondary schools, here and abroad, and another 13 years as a professor in several American universities. His service includes professor of science education, Dean of Education, Campus Dean, as well as an online instructor. His passion for learning (and *how we learn*) did not develop until *after* graduating from high school, and his only explanation for this is that *having a goal made all the difference in the world*. He enjoys reading, hiking, nature photography, golf, and tennis.

http://richardnesmith.obior.cc

Also, visit YouTube's *Educational Videos for Learning,* and *Applied Principles of Education & Learning Publication™.*
https://bit.ly/3fd7prn

Other educational, wildlife, and naturalist books available by **Dr. Richard NeSmith.**

Applied **P**rinciples of **E**ducation & Learning

presents

APE-Learning

AMAZON AUTHOR's PAGE:

https://www.amazon.com/author/richardnesmith

---

[i] Special thanks to the following who kindly provided permission to use their photographs. From unsplash.com (Caleb Martin, Demi Felicia Vares, Dusan Smetana, Embla Munk Rynkebjerg, Jeffrey Hamilton, JP Valer, Kulli Kittus, Nicola Nuttall, and Oguzhan -Akinc). In addition, special thanks to **Molly Bowen**, **Stacey Diamond**, **Rosemary Crosman**, **Cindy Frasier**, **David Peters**, and **Greg Jowers** for wonderful photos. And, as always, special thanks to **Dr. Laurie Aleixo**, for her photographs, her rehab work, and her support and encouragement. Dr. Aleixo's photo made a *wonderful book cover*. And, special thanks to my son, **Wendell C. NeSmith** for his feeding squirrel park photo AND his *invaluable* help in assisting me with much of the producing of these books. *Thank you all.*